Abdul Malek, Ph.D.

THE EINSTEINIAN UNIVERSE?

A DIALECTICAL PERSPECTIVE OF MODERN THEORETICAL PHYSICS AND COSMOLOGY

M100 © Anglo-Australian Observatory
Photo by David Malin

THE EINSTEINIAN UNIVERSE?

A DIALECTICAL PERSPECTIVE OF MODERN THEORETICAL PHYSICS AND COSMOLOGY

ABDUL MALEK, Ph.D.

Agamee Prakashani

First Published: August 2004
Second Edition, December 2015
Published By Agamee Prakashani
36 Banglabazar, Dhaka-1100
E-mail: info@agameeprakashani-bd.com
Cover Design : Masuk Helal
Printed by Swarbarna Printers
18/26/4, Suklal Das Lane, Dhaka
Price:Tk. 250.00/US $ 9.00
Cover: Galaxy M-100
Anglo-Australian Observatory
Photo by David Malin
ISBN : 978 984 04 18251

To my father, whose profound sense of judgment always fascinated me and to *Mejho Bhai*, who was my childhood mentor & a source of inspiration.

"There is nothing permanent except change. Everything changes due to inner strife" Heraclitus

*"Just as there is **no motion without matter**, so there is **no matter without motion**"* G.W.F. Hegel

"How is it that the sky feeds the stars!" Lucretius

*"There is no leap in nature, **precisely because** nature is composed entirely of leaps!"* Frederick Engels

"Space is not something objective and real, nor a substance, nor an accident, nor a relation; instead, it is subjective and ideal, and originates from the mind's nature in accord with a stable law as a scheme, as it were, for coordinating everything sensed externally." Emmanuel Kant

"Since the theory of general relativity (GR) implies the representation of physical reality by a continuous field, the concept of particles and material points cannot play a fundamental part and neither can the concept of motion. The particle can only appear as a limited region in space in which the field strength or energy density is particularly high". Albert Einstein

"The question whether objective truth can be attributed to human thinking is not a question of theory but a practical question. In practice man must prove the truth, i.e., the reality and power, the "this-sidedness" of his thinking.. The dispute over the reality or non-reality of thinking which is isolated from practice is a purely scholastic question". Karl Marx

CONTENTS

Preface to the Second Edition	09
Foreword	13
The Two Opposite World-Outlooks	17
The Natural Science of Monopoly Capitalism	25
Causality and Dialectics	37
The Magic of Mathematics	51
Epilogue	63
Appendix I: A Selected List of Philosophers and Thinkers	67

Preface to the Second Edition

The first edition of this booklet came out in 2004 as a private publication only for limited distribution. It was meant to be a draft "manifesto" or a pamphlet against official natural science. It was meant to be an expression of raw and impulsive reaction at the transparent manipulation and expropriation by monopoly capitalism of high profile scientific research in general and in particular its attempts to make modern physics preach theology. Albert Einstein's theory of General Relativity (GR) has become more or less the Bible of modern official science. Arthur Eddington's well-publicized but questionable claim to have "proven" this theory by measuring the bending of starlight by the sun in 1919 set GR on to the road of glory.

The turn of the 20th century saw few revolutionary developments of unprecedented scale, in natural and social sciences that on the one hand were bound not only to threaten the old social order and paradigm but also at the same time open up great potentials for the future of humanity. The discovery of the theory of evolution (1859) in biology, the quantum phenomena (1900) in physics and the Bolshevik revolution (1917) in Russia were such epoch making developments, which were incompatible with the old paradigm of causality and could only be comprehended through materialist dialectics as a tool developed by Karl Marx and Frederick Engels. The ruling Bourgeois capitalist world system of that time, which was already reeling with internal crises and conflicts of destructive wars, could face these new threats only by transforming itself to regressive and parasitic monopoly capitalism under the leadership of Anglo-American led Western imperialism as a world socio-economic system.

Albert Einstein came as God-sent, to defend the old order that was threatened by these new developments in natural and social sciences. As a reaction to "spooky" quantum phenomenon, and to save the threatened but venerable notions of certainty, continuity, determinism, causality etc. of the old established order, Einstein proposed his theory of general relativity (1915) based on ancient Greek mathematical idealist concept of space and time and the concept of "continuous field" as the objective basis of reality as opposed to the notion of matter in motion of materialism. This theory set a new idealist cosmology in the service of monopoly capitalism, which is very similar to the Ptolemaic "epicycles" and geocentric cosmology of medieval despotism. As Karl Marx said, *"the ruling ideas of an epoch are the ideas of its ruling class"*, so it is no wonder that Einstein would be co-opted as the new prophet, after theology lost much of its appeal.

This also marks the subjective transition of official science from a basis on classical materialism to mathematical idealism - a domination of theory over experiment in physics that henceforth is to become the primary characteristics of "New Physics" under monopoly capitalism. Eddington, as the ideological representative was reported to have said, "Experimental results are valid only if supported by a good theory". This "new edict" of Eddington came in the context of his manipulation of the experimental results of the bending of starlight by the sun to "prove" the prediction of GR. This became the modus operandi of modern theoretical physics. The major preoccupation of modern high-value and subjective experiments is to "prove" the esoteric theories like GR, Big Bang etc. as proof of theological genesis of the universe. "Social practice" as the criteria of positive knowledge was abrogated in favor of subjective "proof" by individual scientists.

Edwin Hubble's "law" relating the redshift of cosmic bodies with distance was purported to have sealed the deal for a Big Bang creation of the universe in conformity with General Relativity and the "first cause" of theology. Subsequent tenuous and subjective experiments in the fields of astro- and particle physics with claims of ever-increasing "precision" are being made to establish the incontrovertible truth of a "theory of everything" - a "final theory" that is supposed to unite GR as the theory of the macrocosm with the equally "precise" Standard Model of the quantum world of the microcosm. This confidence in the triumph of monopoly capitalism in the realm of Nature was boosted by the economic and geo-political victory after the collapse of "communism" in Russia and China by late seventies of 20th century. The extension of its economic and political might all around the world; meant an "end of history". The only sore point was the new revolution in Iran.

The intoxicated euphoria of monopoly capitalism and the intimidation of the working people at the beginning of the new millennium seemed so overwhelming that the publication of a book of this type for a general readership seemed to be an act of sheer lunacy. But the inexorable dialectical development of history and the increase in the positive knowledge in natural sciences in the past few decades makes the publication of a book of this type feasible again. A strong imperative for a formal public edition also came from the enthusiasm shown towards this booklet by a few people to whom it was distributed in 2004; most notably from (Late) Halton (Chip) Arp, when he was associated with the Max-Planck Institute at Garching near Munich in Germany.

The present is also an epoch when monopoly finance capitalism as the last stage of capitalism has reached its terminal point, as its economic crises multiply especially after the decades long wars in the Middle East. The inter-capitalist conflicts are also intensifying with the rise of newly capitalist superpower contenders like China and Russia. The vulnerable revolution in Iran continues to thrive and extend its influence over the Middle East, and the anti-imperialist movements in Latin America continues to gather strength in tandem. Most of all, the dark clouds of uncertainties and bankruptcies gather intensity in the otherwise make-belief bright sky of the theoretical sciences of monopoly capitalism, which so far acted as its prop. But the world is changing, edifices are crumbling, absolute truths are tarnishing at an accelerated rate, as physics at the lead of theoretical natural science continues to evolve at a faster pace. In spite of all attempts to make physics to crown monopoly capitalism with a "theory of everything" and the absolute truth of the creation of the world with a God Particle; it now seems more likely that it will get the exact opposite of what it wished for; because more and more new findings in the realm pf particle and astrophysics by the official physicists themselves are at odd with what they wished to find and the results are unable to reconcile with the bloated claims of their theories.

My decade-long debate on the basis of the dialectical views expressed in this booklet, in the British online newspaper The Guardian as "futurehuman", (particularly in the science Blog "Life and Physics" by Prof. Jon Butterworth) convinced me that there is now a sea-change in the status of official theoretical natural science and cosmology as it now faces intractable contradictions. It now seems that this booklet would not generate as much outrage and hostility towards it as would have been the case back in 2004.

A revision of the booklet would necessitate extensive changes in the content, the format and the style of the text, which would involve major efforts. Also it would change the original perspective with which I viewed cosmology at the formative stage of the development of my own views. For this reason most of the old part of the booklet is left as it was with some minor additions and modifications here and there. Only the Appendix II is omitted in this edition as it now forms a chapter in another published book. An epilogue is added instead, as an update of my present view on the status of official theoretical physics and cosmology. It is hoped that this booklet will help to invigorate the great debates that are transforming modern theoretical sciences and particularly cosmology.

Abdul Malek ,

Montreal, Canada, October 2015

FOREWORD

It was G.W.F. Hegel who first criticized and questioned the continuation of the use of what he called the "metaphysical" mode of thought in natural science, which by his time came to some level of sophistication and differentiation. He proposed *dialectics* or the view of *reason* as the proper tool for acquiring positive knowledge of the world instead of the view of *understanding* and *causality* of old natural philosophy.

Karl Marx, Frederick Engels and V.I. Lenin further developed dialectics to *dialectical materialism* as an all round ideological tool to comprehend the development of nature, man and the mind. These vanguards sharpened the old dialectical tools to help equip the emerging proletariat for its historical task of propelling humanity to a higher stage of advancement. Engels, more than anyone else elaborated the views of dialectics in natural science. Subsequent progress in all areas of terrestrial sciences particularly the biological sciences, the Theory of Evolution and Quantum dynamics vindicated the view that the dialectical laws assert themselves in the development of nature.

But *official* science is still openly hostile to the notions of dialectics and only reluctantly, by the way of exceptions and in isolated cases accepts its role. Once vibrant natural science, which brought in a revolutionary transformation of the human society and of mother earth within a span of few hundred years now finds itself tamed in the servitude of one small class represented by monopoly capital. Gone are the days of the *free thinkers*, the passionate and creative giants who pursued their profession for the mere thirst of knowledge under the most severe conditions and more often under the threat of persecution and death. They are now replaced by troops of conformed *scientist serfs* (paraphrased by the Bengali poet Rabindranath Tagore) who are totally dependent on monopoly capital for their livelihood, career and crafts and who toil mightily to bring out only *expected* and *acceptable* results. Those who dare to disagree with or venture out of the official paradigm are silenced through neglect, isolation and outright persecution. J.B.S. Haldane, Halton Arp are just a few relatively more recent examples.

Even before this total subjugation of natural science, Engels undertook a thorough criticism of *official* natural science of his time from a dialectical standpoint. Causality and British empiricism was the mainstay of natural science then as it is now. Engels' ideas clarified much of the confusion that was rampant in many areas of natural sciences, particularly in mathematics, physics, biology and the Theory of Evolution. He thoroughly refuted the idealist views of one Eugene Dühring on mathematics and on cosmology, the same ghosts that are now being resurrected by the present *official* science.

The views of Engels on cosmology and on later developments in physics were of more restricted scope. But this is due to the state of natural science at his time. Thermodynamics by that time was brought to some level of perfection and Quantum Mechanics, which was to dominate natural science in later years, was all but unknown. Even Einstein's special Theory of Relativity was many years away.

The Laws of Thermodynamics, particularly the Law of Conservation of Energy were accepted as articles of faith. Engels was very much influenced by the concept of entropy and the works of Clausius (1822-1888) and Helmholtz (1821-1831). He was troubled by the view of the eventual *heat death* of the universe as predicted by thermodynamics, when entropy will reach a maximum value by the total conversion of all forms of energy into heat so that no energy will be available for useful work or for the differentiation of motion for all eternity. Engels vehemently rejected the notion of such an outcome because it violates the Laws of Dialectics. He seemed to prefer the idea of an *eternally repeated succession of worlds in infinite time* in which entropy is alternately diminished by some yet unknown natural processes, and the universe gets a new *life* to start another cycle.

It is not the fault of Engels that he could not provide a more forceful dialectical view of the universe, when natural science at that time could only predict a pessimistic end of the universe in a *heat death* and Quantum Mechanics and the subatomic world did not yet even make their appearance.

Attempts have been made in this work to collect together the ideas of Engels on modern theoretical natural science, which are still valid today as ever before and to extrapolate these ideas in the light of more recent developments. This author makes no claim to any originality in thought, the content or the style of presentation of dialectical views on natural science, nor does he pretend to have a mastery of the science subjects dealt with in this work. On the contrary, he admits total indebtedness to Engels, who is quoted extensively throughout this work. Even when Engels is not directly quoted, many expressions used by him were borrowed to impart a greater effect. This was done because no one else can match Engels in the masterly and articulate expression of ideas. It is hoped that this effort will induce more authoritative works in this area.

I got help from too many people and books to name them individually here. In particular I would like to thank Prof. Vijaya Mulay who was the first to patiently go through parts of this work and provided valuable comments and suggestions. Prof. Halton C. Arp of the Max Planck Institute in Germany and Prof. J.V. Narlikar of Inter-University Centre for Astronomy and Astrophysics, Pune, in India were very kind to go through an earlier version of the Chapter on "The Two Opposite World Outlooks". Their comments helped me to reformulate some of the ideas and gave me strength to complete this work.

The success of this effort will depend on whether it could uphold a consistent dialectical point of view and could correctly present the modern scientific concepts it has dealt with. If it failed to do so in any area, the blame lies with this author only.

Abdul Malek

Montreal, September 2001

THE TWO OPPOSITE WORLD-OUTLOOKS

Economic & Socio-Political Basis

In a class society, the functions of the superstructure are geared to and are controlled mainly in the interest of the dominant class. The fate of the particular form and the content of the superstructure are always linked to the rise and fall of the dominant economic class. Modern natural science is no exception.

History shows that every dominant class needs a system of final and absolute truth, which forms the global ideological base and provides the moral/rational justification for its rule. This system of absolute truth is always molded out of the credible raw intellectual materials available at hand. Thus, with the successful expansion of the Roman empire into various parts of Europe, Asia and Africa, the local gods of the indigenous cultures including those of the Romans, became inadequate under the changed socio-economic circumstances and consequently decayed making way for the rise of a more cosmopolitan Christianity. Similarly with the rise of revolutionary bourgeois capitalism in late fifteenth century Europe, a Martin Luther had to arise to reform the old ideology to the needs of the new dominating class. In the same way, by late nineteenth and early twentieth century the once revolutionary capitalism decayed into parasitic and reactionary monopoly finance capitalism, and an omni-present and omniscient personal God lost much of His appeal due to the development of natural science. A new system of absolute truth had to be formulated; theoretical natural science and cosmology was there to fulfill this need. But what is characteristic of all these final, absolute etc. truths is that these systems of 8truth are derived not from the real world, but are always imported from an ethereal realm– a realm that is a fuzzy mental reflection of the real world of that time. The architect of these systems of absolute truth always shifting His head quarter beyond the ever-expanding horizon of positive human knowledge.

Modern theoretical natural science has increasingly taken on an idealist/absolutist theological character and has become a tool in the defense of moribund finance capital. This science has forsaken the great tradition of Copernican-Galilean-Darwinian natural science that was inspired by revolutionary bourgeois capitalism and is now striving to set up a system of awe-inspiring eternal, final, absolute etc. truth to give legitimacy to the notion that natural science has come to a limit and that monopoly capitalism is the ultimate achievement of humanity. The general theory of relativity based mainly on mathematical and aesthetic consideration is purported to have conceived the ultimate reality and the absolute truth of the world. The *big bang* creation of the universe based on the theory of relativity provides a vindication of theological genesis. Therefore, the task of modern natural science like that of theology is to interpret and to reveal the workings of this absolute truth in the details of nature.

Modern *official* theoretical natural science thus stands in the same relation to monopoly capitalism as theology was to feudalism.

The Idealistic Paradigm

Official natural science almost exclusively adopted causality and the idealistic view of nature, requiring the role of a designer-creator and the perpetual mystery of a first cause. Cosmology is being led to a blind alley of sterile absolute truths of beautiful mathematical constructs but which with their fantastic and mysterious implications has no meaning for humanity. Starting from Copernicus, natural science undertook its task of understanding nature from nature itself without invoking the supernatural. The triumphant march of natural science since that time is gradually dispelling the fog of mysticism in most areas of human knowledge. But mathematics and cosmology remains the last stronghold of idealism in natural science. Modern theoretical natural science is replete with supernatural categories, the ethereal realm of Plato, the unknowable *thing-in-itself* of Kant etc. Thus we have the new ether (space-time), the big bang origin of the universe, multi-dimensional realities; infinite universes, hyperspace etc. which mankind has no hope of ever having any knowledge of, or of making a definite empirical verification, because these follow from *mathematical consistency* only. But long ago, philosophy in the person of Hegel (an idealist himself) thoroughly refuted these ethereal categories. It is self contradictory to say that the *unknowable* exists. If we have no hope of ever knowing a thing, there is no sense of talking about it! The word *existence* has no meaning except the possibility of its being an object to consciousness.

Dialectical Perspective

But historically, the idealistic view that everything in this world was created at one stroke *perfect in-itself*, that nature has extension in space and only undergoes cyclic changes but has no successive stages of *development* in time, is not the only notion that man had of nature. Almost simultaneously the opposite, the dialectical view of nature as something 'that comes into being and passes out of existence, as something eternally changing and developing in successive stages' - also arose with early civilizations and in the most developed form with the Greeks. A dialectical view of the world is always inimical to any established order or a class-based society, because this view prohibits any finality of knowledge or attainment of any absolute truth and it denies any stability of a thing or a process for all time to come; it allows only temporary stages of evolution in an eternal process of change. The history of theoretical natural science of the last few thousand years is a condemnation of the partial masquerading as the complete; the final and absolute truth always proving to be false. According to dialectics mankind is doomed forever to deal only with partial, incomplete and relative truths in an ever-developing series brought on by successive generations, without ever reaching one final or absolute truth. It however recognizes the possibility that giant strides can be made from one generation to the next.

Modern theoretical natural science based mostly on mathematics, foists an idealistic view on nature at a time when its experience during the last few centuries including the most recent developments in quantum dynamics, astrophysics, thermodynamics, paleontology, biology and all other terrestrial sciences, points to a nature that is in eternal motion of evolution, development, change, brought about through a conflict of the opposites residing together in its elements, and that although at narrow particularity cause and effect has a role, at all levels of generality it is governed by blind chance events, but with the iron necessity that is inherent in chance. These results are in accordance with the brilliant intuition of the early dialectical thinkers starting from Heraclitus and the subsequent extensions of dialectics by Kant, Hegel, Marx, Engels and Lenin.

Monopoly capital attempts to engrave Einstein's General Theory of Relativity on the face of all eternity as the final and ultimate truth and to put a permanent seal on further human knowledge, with the complete understanding of the big bang creation of the universe. Monopoly capitalism clearly shares this illusion with all the other classes that preceded it. Einstein's theory of gravity must patently be false in the same sense that Newton's theory and all other previous scientific theories were false. One is permitted to come to this conclusion from the consideration of dialectics alone, because according to this science, it is impossible to have a system of knowledge that has unlimited and unconditional validity for all eternity. All profound theories in the past did not put an end to knowledge, but on the contrary enlarged its boundaries. Darwin wrote of his theory of evolution: *"How wide and rich a field for study has been opened up through the principle of evolution and such without the light shed on them by this principle would for a long time or for ever have remained barren"*[1]

One must not forget that it was a dialectical philosopher, Emanuel Kant and not a scientist who first laid the scientific basis to cosmology. Had science been constrained by the Newtonian absolute truth of the *harmonious* and perpetual motion of the heavenly bodies after an initial divine push, it is doubtful whether astronomy would have progressed so far as it is today. Kant's epoch-making insight into *cosmic evolution* has helped science to understand in the most general and broadest outline, the *evolution* and *development* of nature from the galaxies to its highest product – the rationally thinking brain and the thread running through the intermediate links. The same basic thread of dialectical thought must be followed if one has to gain further understanding of the universe and nature. The *big bang* theory of one single act of the creation of the universe must also be false, not only

---

1. Darwin, Charles, "Prefatory Notice: Studies in the Theory of Decent", Sampson Low, London, pp-V-VI. (1882).

because it is infected with the mystery of an unknowable first cause, the empirical verification of which will always be impossible; but also because *"...there is no leap in nature" as Engels said, "**precisely because** nature is composed entirely of leaps."*[2]

In the light of the present development of quantum dynamics, it is probably possible to extend the intuitive ideas of early dialectical thinkers and those of Hegel, and to look at the universe as a process, as something that *comes into being and passes out of existence*. If one naively assumes the universe to be an infinite void in which matter spontaneously *comes into being* in the form of some fundamental particles from *nothing* and similarly vanishes into *nothing* in the literary sense of the first Hegelian triad of *being-nothing-becoming* then there must always be some finite matter in the universe, because Uncertainty Principle forbids a perfect vacuum. Further, if this spontaneous appearance and disappearance of matter is an eternal and everyday phenomena of innumerable *free lunches* instead of the quantum mechanically less feasible one-time mighty *big bang free lunch*, then the dialectical view of the universe becomes realistic and all of these fantastic mathematics and awe inspiring modern cosmology of genesis becomes unnecessary. If the appearance and disappearance of matter is facilitated, so to speak catalyzed by the presence of existing matter as the graininess of the universe suggests and as quantum electrodynamics indicates the increasing concentration of virtual particles close to an atomic nucleus, and if such matter particles collects (like water molecules in the cloud) under the attractive force of gravity to form nebulae, galaxies, stars and so on then we can appreciate the anticipating poetic wonderment of Lucretius: *"How is it that the sky feeds the stars!"*[3] Unlike the idealistic notion of *official* science, gravity cannot be only an attractive force, but according to the dialectical law of the *unity of the opposites*, must also possess a repulsive nature If the repulsive force

---

2. Engels, F. "Dialectics of Nature", Translated and Edited by Clemens Dutt, International Publishers, p. 318 (1940).

3. Quoted in "The Universe Beyond", Dickinson, Terence, 3rd. ed. Firefly Books Ltd. Buffalo, N.Y., (1999).

of gravity at long distance overwhelms the relatively short-range attractive force, then the general dispersion of matter as observed by Hubble and the acceleration of this dispersion as observed recently, can be explained without invoking a primordial push from a *Big Bang*.

The speculation about the creation and disappearance of matter as elementary particle, if true, must involve both matter and anti-matter. If in one tiny region of the infinite void, matter gets pre-eminence over anti-matter by purely chance events but with a necessity that chance entails, then the development of an island universe like the one in which we live in to be composed of only matter is perfectly feasible, because any new anti-matter that forms is continuously eliminated through reaction with existing matter by the well known annihilation process, producing γ-rays, – a sort of *natural selection* as is the case in the biological systems. The energy created this way and through other processes must decay during its lifetime to form a background radiation or so to speak, some *zero-point* energy also mandated by quantum mechanics. This *zero-point* energy can represent the cosmic microwave background radiation, which is touted by *official* science as the *fingerprint of God* and the incontrovertible proof of the *big bang* theory.

If such a simple picture of the universe is correct then it will be similar to the development of galaxies, solar systems and life or other processes in terrestrial nature, in all of which science so far has found to follow dialectical laws of development. This naïve but essentially correct way of looking at the world by the early dialectical thinkers, (and which can be perceived by any individual with some reflection), is being more and more reinforced with the development of natural science. It is possible to comprehend the infinite universe by studying the finite nature, because according to dialectics the infinite (the self-limited) lies in the finite – is the finite. As Engels said: *"The extreme limit of our natural science until now has been our universe, and we do not need the infinitely numerous universes outside it to obtain knowledge of nature. Indeed, only a single sun among millions, with its solar system, forms the essential basis of our astronomical researches"*[4]

But such a simple rendering of the matter as complex as the universe must be viewed with horror, ridicule and utter contempt by the state appointed theoretical scientists and cosmologists who have come under the total domination of monopoly capital and make a living by mastering brain-wrecking mathematics! *Official* natural science must first of all have a mechanism to limit space and time, because it does not have the tools to deal with infinity, any more than old materialism could bridge the gap between the finite and the infinite. If infinites do indeed appear in its equations, then these must be eliminated by some arbitrary mathematical tricks such as renormalizations. The only way, they can widen their horizon is by climbing another rung of new mathematics. If in the process of climbing they find few holes and gaps in the picture then they must wait for a messiah, a genius in mathematics who will help them to form the next rung and so on. But mathematical relations like all other theoretical knowledge are abstractions from empirical experience. As Engels and Lenin always emphasized, all abstractions when pushed beyond their limits are transformed into nonsense or into their opposites.

In their lonely climb on the ladder of mathematics and causality, the theoretical scientists claim to have reached close to the very top from where they will be able to see everything there is to be seen and will be ready to announce to the world the final, ultimate and the absolute truth and humanity will then *know the mind of God*. Although many gaps and holes remains in their picture and new ones constantly appear as they attempt to build the few final rungs, they are confident that the *mathematical consistency* will carry them through to the top. But the only problem is that except for its use by monopoly capital to induce awe and reverence in the general populace, this final truth will have no other meaning to the lesser mortals on earth, and the only way for these theoreticians to ever come closer to conventional science again, is by crashing down through the high virtual edifice that they have so painfully constructed.

So what in the final analysis is the future prospect of life and consciousness in this universe – a question that resides at the core of the heart of us all? Predictably enough, our evangelical *official*

---

4. Engels, F. "Dialectics of Nature", Translated and Edited by Clemens Dutt, International Publishers, p. 164 (1940).

cosmology provides a grim prognosis –a sort of doomsday indeed:- depending on some measurable parameters, the universe will either collapse back to the size of a proton crushing us and everything else with it, thus reversing the process of creation (this cycle may be repeated if the creator so wishes), or it will keep on expanding (at predictable rates) with the helpless humans watching in horror as they are torn away from their familiar neighbouring galaxies and life will be lost for ever in a continually-expanding space-time etc. etc. This impels us to bow our head in all humility and reverence not only to the creator, but also to the experts who are in the know of His cosmic design!

In the words of Halton Arp: "*Monopoly capitalism vs. desire for knowledge and curiosity about how we and the world works. Fear vs. courage. Is our historical base line long enough to know which will prevail? The galaxies and quasars make me somewhat hopeful*"[5]

And most of all, one should always remember the passionate and dialectical assessment of Engels:"*... however many millions of suns and earths may arise and pass away, however long it may last before the conditions for organic life develop, however innumerable the organic beings that have to arise and pass away before animals with a brain capable of thought are developed from their midst, and for a short span of time find conditions suitable for life, only to be exterminated later without mercy, we have the certainty that matter remains eternally the same in all its transformations, that none of its attributes can ever be lost, and therefore also, that with the same iron necessity that it will exterminate on the earth its highest creation, the thinking mind, it must somewhere else and at another time again produce it.*"[6]

---

5. Arp, H., personal communications, September, (2001).

6. Engels, F., "Dialectics of Nature"; Translated and Edited by Clemens Dutt, International Publishers, p. 24- 25 (1940).

THE NATURAL SCIENCE OF MONOPOLY CAPITALISM

In an age of specialization in its extreme, for a non-expert to write on a subject of this nature seems to be an act of *sacrilegium*. Yet, I have ventured to undertake such an enterprise in the fashion of a Don Quixote, with the full awareness that this work will at best be ridiculed by any representative of the *official* science who cares to take notice of this at all! But again, the present state of theoretical natural science provoked me to undertake such a thankless task.

Theoretical natural science has now reached a state in which Pythagoras comes back with vengeance. Yet once again natural science is able to know the secrets of nature and the laws that govern her, by means of thought alone and by the power of aesthetics & mathematics, without the recourse to experimentation or empirical experience. Albert Einstein the greatest scientist of the twentieth century contrasts his new notion of physics with those of Copernicus, Kepler, Galileo etc., in the following way [1]:

"The natural philosophers of those days were on the contrary most of them possessed with the idea that fundamental concepts and postulates of physics were not in the logical sense free inventions of the human mind but could be deduced from experience by abstraction – that is to say by logical means. A clear recognition of the erroneousness of this notion really came with the general theory of relativity,"

It is a pity that Professor Einstein was not born centuries ago; with his *free invention of human mind* he could have saved humanity from suffering the pains of the tortuous scientific development of the last few thousand years! It therefore, follows that any person who is capable of thinking at all, is in a position to make a statement on the ultimate truth of the universe as a democratic right!

---

1. A. Einstein, "Essays in Science", Translated by Alan Harris from "Mein Weltbild, Quedro Verlag, Amsterdam, (1933), The Wisdom Library, N.Y., p. 48 – 49 (1934).

The only difference between a professional and a layperson it would seem lies in the fact that a professional expert can dress up his or her opinion in beautiful mathematics while a lay person cannot. Mathematics is a vast storehouse of nifty little things, where a lucky one can enter if he or she has the keys and pick up items with which to decorate their theories. With the wizardry of mathematics you can incorporate a fudge factor, choose boundary conditions or make assumptions by which you can eliminate the infinities and unwanted solutions of an equation, *et voila*, you obtain the results you wanted to get at the first place. You choose to apply mathematics only to those areas of science that are amenable to mathematical treatment and then you wonder in amazement at *the Unreasonable Effectiveness of Mathematics in the Natural Sciences* But now a days even that is not a sure thing. You can have a theory based on impeccable mathematics and still you get nowhere. In the language of Physicist Freeman Dyson [2], *"The ground of physics is littered with the corpses of unified theories"*. The same is true for cosmology also.

If the requirements of empirical verification and the practical means of doing so were necessary conditions of a good theory in Copernican mechanics, this is no longer the case now. As science extends more and more in the realm of the microcosm and macrocosm, the practicality of experimentation and empirical verification of theories become limited and/or unreliable. On the other hand because of the very nature of the *"official"* philosophy of modern science, one becomes tempted to search for the ultimate truth of the world by the power of thought and aesthetics alone. Mathematics is there, like theology before it, as the handmaiden to do this miracle.

Thus natural science comes back one full circle from the Copernican revolution to theology again and falls on its knees in guilt seeking redemption for having deserted it! And this is necessarily so, because *official* science never broke loose of the iron chain of causality around its neck. Determinism and causality continued to rule natural science even after its liberation from the authority of the church. For old

---

2. F. Dyson, "Disturbing the Universe", Harper & Row, N.Y., p. 62 (1979).

materialism, only what it can explain on the basis of cause and effect is science, the rest belongs to the realm of the creator. Every time a new or unknown phenomenon is encountered, most scientists are quick to invoke the supernatural, thus phlogiston, electricity, ether etc. to name a few were such extra material things. We have our own share of extra material entities, such as dark matter/energy, space-time, hyperspace and multi dimensional reality etc.

So in the final analysis, a recognized expert in theoretical science is no better off than an absolute layman when it comes to finding the *theory of everything*, especially at a time when most of the theoretical scientists are driven back in their hordes to theology again, - a theology whose hands are still stained with the blood of some of the finest sons that natural science ever produced!

The second and more serious sacrilegious thing I have done is to invoke the writings of Frederick Engels. In fact my contribution in this work lies merely in collecting and reproducing the selected writings of Engels regarding the subject at hand. The names of Marx and Engels are anathema to present established world order of Monopoly Capital and of *official* science in particular. If any reference to Marx or Engels brought a forced yawn among the professional scientists before, it brings out-right ridicule now, especially after the defeat of the Khruschevite *"communism"** in Russia and elsewhere in the world. But a science, which after all brought more than half of the world under its influence even if for a short period cannot be so easily dismissed by ridicule alone, nor the least by pretending to ignore its existence altogether.

The total bankruptcy of modern theoretical science should impel the scientists to at least consider the teachings of Engels and dialectical materialism. Engels more than Marx elaborated dialectical materialism especially in the areas of natural science. In his lucid and

---

* So much is the sense of certainty of vanquished "communism" that, now (September, 2000) Canadian television zestfully plays "The International" as part of a commercial advertisement!

inimitable way Engels described the most difficult concepts in such clarity of thought that even his ideological adversaries showed admiration for him. Engels' writings show that he was head and shoulder far above his contemporary scientists of nineteenth century in the theoretical mastery of the vast scientific material that was accumulating at an accelerated rate.

A casual reading of *Dialectics of Nature* and/or *Anti-Dühring* will convince any scientist of the profound understanding by Engels of the essence of science, its historical development and its future course and his comprehensive vision of the interconnectedness, the motion, change and the development of nature from the microcosm to the macrocosm. J.B.S. Haldane[3] who along with Alexander Oparin laid the foundation of the theory of the origin of life wrote of Engels in 1939: *"Had Engels', method of thinking been more familiar, the transformation of our ideas on physics which occurred during the last thirty years would have been smoother. Had his remarks on Darwinism been generally known, I for one would have been saved a certain amount of muddled thinking."*

Engels [4] himself had this to say to the natural scientists in 1885: *"It is however precisely the polar antagonisms put forward as irreconcilable and insoluble, the forcibly fixed lines of demarcation and distinctions between classes, which have given modern theoretical natural science its restricted and metaphysical character The recognition that these antagonisms and distinctions are in fact to be found in nature, but only with relative validity, and that on the other hand this imagined rigidity and absoluteness have been introduced into nature only by our minds – this recognition is the kernel of the dialectical conception of nature. It is possible to reach this standpoint because the accumulating facts of natural science compel us to do so; but we reach it more easily if we approach the dialectical character of these facts equipped with the consciousness of the laws of the dialectical thought. In any case natural science has now advanced so*

---

3. J.B.S. Haldane, "Preface" to "Dialectics of Nature" by F. Engels, International Publishers, N.Y. (1940).

4. F. Engels, "Herr Eugen Dühring's Revolution in Science (Anti Dühring), International Publishers N.Y., p. 19 (1939)

far that it can no longer escape the dialectical synthesis. But it will make this process easier for itself if it does not lose sight of the fact that the results in which its experiences are summarized are concepts; but that the art of working with concepts is not inborn and also is not given with ordinary everyday consciousness, but requires real thought, and that this thought similarly has a long empirical history, not more and not less than empirical natural science. Only by learning to assimilate the results of the development of philosophy during the past two and a half thousand years will it be able to rid itself on the one hand of any isolated natural philosophy standing apart from it, outside it and above it, and on the other hand also of its own limited method of thought, which was its inheritance from English empiricism." How true it is today even after more than a century!

The ideas of Marx and Engels like those of fellow dialecticians Hegel and Kant before them foreshadowed many of the scientific discoveries of nineteenth and twentieth century. Kant's epoch making theory of *cosmic evolution* marked the point of departure from the Newtonian science of *first impulse*, determinism and causality. This brilliant insight demonstrated in a concrete way the validity of the early Greek dialectical thinkers that *everything in this world comes into being and passes out of existence, is in constant motion of change and development*. It was shown for the first time that nature has a history, not only of coexistence in space but also of succession in time. The idealist notion that *everything was created at one stroke, equally perfect in itself* and that *things exist in parallel to each other and not following one another* was shattered once and for all.

But natural science totally ignored Kant. It went about its devious and random ways of twists and turns, cause and effect; with isolated and accidental discoveries, innumerable deviations in false directions and in laboured investigations. About four centuries after Kant's discovery, natural science has pieced together in its broadest outline the landscape of the world envisioned by him – a world in which evolution reins supreme, ranging from the formation of the galaxies to the thought process of man. The great discovery of the evolution of species by Darwin brought crowning success for the dialectical view of nature. The development of quantum dynamics is the strongest vindication of the superiority of dialectical materialism over classical materialism or *Metaphysics* as Hegel termed it.

Quantum dynamics, along with astronomy, thermodynamics, molecular biology, palaeontology, etc. collectively reveal that the laws governing the transformation of matter and life are statistical in character, are shaped by chance and necessity and are not deterministic as assumed by old philosophy. What causality is to Newtonian Mechanics so is dialectics to Quantum dynamics.

Official theoretical natural scientists with their mantra of *"cause and effect"* throw their arms in the air in despair over the results obtained by quantum dynamics, yet it poses no difficulties from the point of view of dialectics. Science has developed to the extent that it cannot pretend to continue any more with old materialism and is forced even if reluctantly to accept the notions of dialectical thought. Ironically, the most violent resistance to this change came from Albert Einstein, – a scientist whose discoveries contributed the most in undoing the basis of the old scientific outlook.

In Einstein's own words[5]: *"Many physicists maintain - and there are weighty arguments in their favour – that in the face of these facts (quantum mechanical), not merely the differential law, but the law of causation itself - hitherto the ultimate basic postulate of all natural science – has collapsed"*

The American mathematician and philosopher P.W. Bridgman[6] laments with a heavy heart that the quantum principle mean: *"nothing more nor less than that the law of cause and effect must be given up, the world is not a world of reason, understandable by the intellect of man"*.

It is precisely this principle of causality that brought pre-Hegelian philosophy and modern theoretical science to this impasse and in a blind alley. The old philosophy tried to understand and explain the world by finding a cause for it. It was totally incapable of deducing categories from one another, of explaining motion, change & development in the world without ascribing a first impulse from God. If the universe has a cause, then either that cause is an effect of a prior

---

5. A. Einstein, "Essays in Science", p. 38-39 (1934)

6. Quoted in C. Suplee Ed., "Physics in the 20th Century", N.H. Adams Inc. N.Y., p. 88 (1999).

cause or it is not. Either the chain of cause & effect extends back to an infinite series or one has to terminate it at some point with a first cause. In either case the first cause will remain unexplained and hence a mystery. To take an example, even if Professors Einstein, Hawking and similar other supermen of the past, present and the future can explain the origin of the universe in the finest details up to the millionth of a second after the *Big Bang,* from the principle of causality, the question as to why and how the *"big bang"* occurred will still be a mystery, because it is the effect of a cause which is unexplained and inexplicable. And so this way no absolute and ultimate truth is ever obtainable, except by invoking the finger of our well-known God. Thomas Aquinas (1224-1274) saw this very clearly long time ago and it was the basis of his "cosmological proof" of the existence of God.

Yet causality was the first casualty of Hegelian philosophy. Hegel's (1770-1831) dialectics came as a rude shock to the otherwise serene world of cause and effect and the Aristotelian notions of identity, contradiction and the excluded middle.

Hegel brought back the dialectics of Heraclitus and came out with the seemingly absurd proposition of the *unity of the opposites*, that "a thing both *is* and *something else* at the same time", that *things and their mental images – ideas, develop due to the conflict of the opposites inherent in them through the triple movement of thesis, antithesis and synthesis*. For Hegel, opposites reside in the same element and therefore, are in a contradiction. Because logic cannot rest in contradiction, it must be resolved in a synthesis. The synthesis is a development but in turn becomes a new thesis itself because it contains the elements of unity and the opposition of the parent contradiction, and emergent new ones of its own and so on. With his law of the *negation of negation* Hegel showed that nothing in this world is eternal and absolute, except for the fact that everything is in a flux of change, in eternal motion. So there can never be any final, absolute and ultimate truth for all time to come.

Hegel characterized his philosophy as the view of *reason* and contrasted it with the view of *"understanding"* of old philosophy. *Understanding* meets every question with an inflexible *either ...or*; the truth is either A or not-A. *Reason* breaks up this hard and fast rule of *understanding*, sees that A and not-A are identical in their very difference; that the truth does not lie, as *understanding* supposes, *either* wholly in A, *or* wholly in not-A, but rather in the synthesis of the two. In other words, for *understanding* A and not-A are *either* identical *or* different; for *reason* they are *both* identical and different at the same time. As an example, an electron according to classical mechanics must either be a particle or a wave. But depending on the experimental set up it can be shown that the electron behaves both as a particle and a wave. This wave-particle duality, Uncertainty Principle and other quantum phenomena are absurd and incomprehensible for classical mechanics but poses no difficulty for quantum dynamics and are in conformity with the Hegelian dialectics

What we observe in *official* theoretical natural science is exactly the opposite of the Hegelian notion of the world. On the one hand there is confusion, puzzlement, disbelief, and despair over the results obtained by quantum dynamics and on the other, there is an attempt to bring a closure, a sort of finality to our knowledge of the universe. While in religion and in philosophy humanity enjoys the comfortable and cozy notion of absolute truth and certainty, natural science so far has been clumsy; has explained the world only superficially, and now quantum dynamics threatens to banish certitude and absolute truth from the realm of nature all together. This is scandalous! Natural science has followed a wrong path, since the time of Plato. Now at last *official* science has found the magic tools – the power of mathematics and symmetry with which to pry open the secrets of the universe and find the final absolute truth.

It is remarkable that just at a time when quantum dynamics - a tool of unprecedented precision, has offered convincing proof (what thermodynamics and statistical mechanics had already indicated before) that all laws of nature are only statistical laws that gives an incomplete, overall, and average knowledge of a *collection of a large number of individual particles and processes*, that *official* science finds it necessary to hurriedly establish certainty and finality of knowledge and nail a board across any further progress.

The development of natural science during the past few centuries has been greatly influenced by the typical English empiricism and narrow-minded opportunism of *"enlightened self-interest"* as England gained dominance in economic and colonial power during the industrial revolution in Europe. By early twentieth century, specially after a series of inter-capitalist wars, bourgeois capitalism transformed into monopoly finance capitalism, under Anglo-American domination. As the economic, political and military domination increased, so did the necessity for the control of the practice of science and technology and the need of an all-encompassing ideology. Since religion, by this time lost much of its influence, monopoly capitalism found in Einstein's theory of general relativity an opportunity to form a system of absolute truth that will provide it credible moral authority. In the year 1919, Arthur Eddington, a prominent representative of British monopoly capitalism claimed to have proven Einstein's theory by an experiment on the bending of starlight by the sun, even though later calculations using his experimental data did not support such a conclusion, a phenomena which Stephan Hawking[7] described as: *"a case of knowing the result they wanted to get, not an uncommon occurrence in science"*. Eddington thus initiated for the first time the trend of credible manipulation as a part of *enlightened self-interest* in the field of natural science also, as fundamental research became an exclusive domain for monopoly capitalism. Needless to say this principle of *enlightened self-interest* of old materialism was a powerful tool in the hands of the British imperial authority in political, economic, military etc. fields.

The classical materialism of causality tasted its decisive defeat with Darwin's theory of evolution, as hostility to this theory continues till today. In spite of its manipulated and official direction, the development of natural science slowly riddled the platform of old materialism with holes and now quantum dynamics has taken away completely the platform from under its feet.
Driven away from most mainstream branches of science, old materialism is taking recourse to repellent faith and is now shifting its head quarter in the mystical clouds of mathematics and in the distant reaches of the cosmos.

---

7. S. Hawking, "A Brief History of Time", Bantam Books, p. 32 (1990).

For, *free creation of the mind*, cause & effect, the absolute beauty of symmetry and mathematics etc. can only manifest themselves in the Platonic realm of perfect order, beauty and static reality. The real world of motion, change and development is too chaotic, vulgar and unpredictable for the beauty of symmetry and mathematics to function. This world is the broken heap of the Platonic realm of perfect beauty and order. The task of modern theoretical natural science is to piece together these broken shards to the original reality and thereby to arrive at the final absolute truth of the universe.

With the acumen of a village priest or a TV evangelist who describes in authoritative details how through a primordial thunder God created the world, *official* cosmology can explain in second by second details the evolution of the universe after it emerged from an initial *"big bang"* about 14 billion years ago and is expanding ever since. The universe had no past – not even the very notion of the *past*. It offers only three possibilities of the future of the universe, depending on the values of some measurable parameters; humanity and all else that has existence are doomed to be within a closed universe with no boundary and there is nothing out side or even the notion of *out side*. Space-time and matter or anything else were, all created by a designer supreme being in one go. Everything is destined to follow a predetermined and harmonious extension in space-time, and is the realization in detail of the primordial mathematical design. For a believer this is overwhelming. One cannot but have awe, reverence and absolute amazement at not only these facts but also the persons who have knowledge of these facts!

The mystical authority of the supernatural, coupled with direct physical force has been the main tools of domination in human society throughout the ages. It took different forms suited to the class structure in different epoch. But mystery always sets up its kingdom outside the horizon of positive knowledge and recedes further as the sphere of scientific knowledge increases. Implicit in this mysticism is the notion that the persons in know of these facts have some special link with God or the supernatural being and therefore deserves special authority, privilege and respect. It definitely helps the cause of *official* natural science when the Vatican patronizes the mystical notion of *big bang* theory and when one of the most famous scientist of twentieth century had a saint like feature and another one (unfortunately) has lost virtually all means of communication with the world except for the waggling of a computer button. It is as if God is speaking through them. But the history of the development of natural science during the last few centuries clearly shows that no mystery exists in nature; behind all apparent mysteries lay human ignorance and fantasy.

Modern cosmologist claim near complete understanding of the universe with the knowledge of (by their own account) only about 4% of its matter, with absolutely no idea whether "dark matter/energy" and "space-time" which are supposed to affect or is affected by matter comes under the concept of *matter* at all! But this, in no way deter the theoretical scientists from pronouncing the imminent discovery of the *"theory of everything"* or from finding the final and the absolute truth of the universe. Strangely enough no absolute truth is claimed in the areas which are close to home or at least are amenable to easy and direct investigation, for example in biological and other terrestrial sciences or the colossal impoverishment and pauperization of the vast majority of the world population by monopoly capitalism. Hand in hand with the complete knowledge of the universe & its creator, we have the absolute truth that humanity can attain ultimate self-realization only by being a "perfect consumer". Monopoly capitalism, which alone has triumphed over past tribalism, feudalism, rural idiocy in integrating the whole world under its rule, and has "defeated" its budding future enemy i.e., *communism* – is the ultimate that humanity can hope for.

Thus the role of modern science is to develop a myth and an all encompassing *system* of absolute knowledge of the world, through which monopoly capital will establish eternal rule over humanity – a state of perfect social, political, economic and ideological order, which will eliminate all conflicts and change of any kind except those occurring in nature, in one word bringing an *end of history*. The universities are to become the supreme authority on knowledge and the final truth, replacing the moribund church, nay, becoming the church itself in intimidating the working people with an air of reverence, awe and mystery. Modern academia stands in the same relation to monopoly capitalism as the clergy was to the feudal aristocracy.

It is no wonder that the gentlemen in theoretical natural science who boastfully proclaim that, they are very close to finding the *theory of everything*, and the apologists of monopoly capital who gleefully declare "the end of science and the end of history" should choose to react so violently towards quantum dynamics and dialectical thinking, or choose to ignore its existence all together. Curiously enough, there is a ring of dialectical truth in this proclamation. It is an honest recognition of the fact that capitalism has reached its limit, it can go no further and is ripe for its demise.

It was by the mid nineteenth century that the working class developed and matured enough in the womb of capitalism to clearly formulate its new world outlook based on dialectical materialism and put forward a concrete program to take the leadership of humanity and propel it further ahead. This task remain largely unfulfilled and as a result, the stale water of monopoly capital has given way to an overgrowth of wild weeds in all areas of human knowledge including natural science. Quantum dynamics, which was inspired by dialectical thinking, still remains a curiosity. Either a total bankruptcy of modern natural science will lead to a new scientific revolution, or a working class revolution will put an end to this idealist rubbish of monopoly capitalism.

CAUSALITY AND DIALECTICS

We are in no way concerned here with the writing of a scholarly dissertation about philosophy, but only to briefly recap the history of the development of these ideas.

Natural Philosophy begins at the stage of the development of the society when human beings starts to try to explain the world & the happenings in nature by ascribing to some causes inherent in nature as opposed to the belief of myth, magic or religion, which attributed things as the doings of some extra-material or extraordinary power or spirit.

Thus philosophy like all other things in the world begins as a dialectical process, with the *"great basic question: which is primary, spirit or nature – that question, in relation to the church, was sharpened into this: 'Did God create the world or has the world been in existence eternally?' The answer, which the philosophers gave to this question, split them into two great camps. Those who asserted the primacy of spirit to nature, and therefore, in the last instance assumed world creation in some form or other,...comprised the camp of idealism. The others, who regarded nature as primary, belong to the various schools of materialism"*[1]. Philosophy developed through the interplay of these two opposite modes of thought.

Interwoven in this process of philosophical development were two general outlooks – one that saw the world and the things in it as absolutely immutable, created *'perfect in themselves'* at one stroke and once for all, as final, unchanging and fixed objects only unfolding in space but not developing in time. Any change, development or motion in this view is due to an *impulse* from an external agency and is governed by the laws of *cause* and *effect*.

The opposed outlook that considered everything as a process, as unstable, eternally changing, as *'coming into being and passing out of*

---

1. F. Engels, "Ludwig Feuerbach and the Outcome of Classical German Philosophy", International Publishers, N.Y., p. 21 (1941).

existence'; due to the conflict of the opposites inherent in itself and residing in its own element. These two opposite outlooks were termed by Hegel as the view of *understanding* (or metaphysics) and the view of *reason* (or dialectics) respectively.

From the narrower perspective of natural science and for the purpose of this discussion these two outlooks may be expressed as causality and dialectics. In a crude sense, causality may be associated with determinism and continuity of classical mechanics while dialectics can be identified with probability, uncertainty and discreteness of quantum dynamics. At the popular level, these two outlooks get their reflection, on the one hand, in the conservative fundamentalism and bourgeois individualism, which believe that things, people and events are uniquely determined, and on the other hand, the liberal and the socialistic views, where the role of the circumstances and that of the environment are emphasized.

The manifestation of these two opposite tendencies is apparent even among the earliest philosophers, specially, among the Greek thinkers. Thus Parmenides (515-450 B.C.) denied, *becoming*. For him *being* is the fullness of all that exists. *"Being cannot come from non-being or be reduced to non-being"*[2].

Heraclitus (544-483 B.C.) on the contrary saw the world as a process – as changing all the time: *"Nothing in this world of ours just permanently is. Things come into existence in their different ways, are never the same for two moments together so long they exist, until eventually they go out of existence again. Everything in the universe is like it – perhaps the universe itself is like it. ...Things are like flames. Flames look as if they are objects, but they are not so much objects as processes"* [3].

Heraclitus, also formulated the idea of the *unity of the opposites*: *"Everything is coming together of opposites or at least of opposite tendencies. ...If you do away with contradiction you would do away with reality; but this in turn means that reality is inherently unstable. Everything is in flux all the time, **everything is flux**"*[4]. These two

---

2. Quoted in Ian P. McGreal Ed., "Great Thinkers of the Western World", HarperCollin Publishers Inc, p. 03 (1992).
3. B. Magee, "The Story of Philosophy: The Essential Guide to the History of Western Philosophy", The Reader's Digest Association (Canada) Ltd., Montreal, p. 14-15 (1998).
4. Ibid, p. 14 (1998)

aspects of the philosophy of Heraclitus – the dynamic nature of reality and the *unity of the opposites*, form the kernel of the dialectical perspective of the world.

The history of the development of philosophy in Europe from the ancient Greeks and Italians, to the Rationalists, to the British Empiricists, the French Free Thinkers, through to the German Idealists has been a conflict of the opposites, a dialectical interplay of idealism and materialism, a see-saw process of the predominance of the one or the other, culminating in Hegel. This process was impelled and pushed forward by the new contents achieved through the rapidly increasing advancement of science and technology, which in turn enriched both idealism and materialism.

After Plato had formulated it in an all round way, idealism thrived all along through theological scholasticism and continues to flourish in the various vulgarized form of professorial philosophy and *official* natural science. George Berkeley, David Hume and German Idealists, specially, Hegel were the important later proponents of idealism.

The great Greek materialism (of Heraclitus, Leucippus, Democritus, and Epicurous) was eclipsed in Europe during the fundamentalist Christian medieval period; until through an indirect reflection from the Muslim Arabs, materialism found its shine and revival again in Europe of the fifteenth century. Materialism advanced in great strides along with the development of natural science during the bourgeois democratic revolution in Europe and found its highest development in the dialectical materialism of Karl Marx.

The view of *understanding* (or metaphysics) and the view of *reason* (or dialectics) had a history of development similar and parallel to that of idealism and materialism. These dialectically related tendencies *metaphysics* and *dialectics* existed simultaneously side by side in the same epoch represented by different personalities and some times as in the case of Aristotle and Kant, in the same person. Until Hegel, both idealism and materialism were mainly guided by *metaphysics* or causality.

A selected list of the important personalities in the critical epochs in the history of the development of Nature- philosophy in Europe is shown in the Appendix I.
Causality reached its perfection with Aristotle (384-322 BC) who also had analyzed the basic forms of dialectical thinking. His notion of **identity, contradiction** and the **excluded middle**, ruled philosophy until Hegel and it never ceased to rule *official* natural science even more than a hundred year after quantum dynamics has demolished its foundation.

As Werner Heisenberg [5] rightly points out, the approach of atomic physics, statistical mechanics and chemistry, starting from the early atomicists such as Leucippus & Democritus were very different from that of determinism, causality and classical mechanics; it was in essence dialectical. Leucippus and Democritus conceived all things as temporary and dynamic structures composed of individual particles or atoms and all processes as the statistical combinations of many small individual events. This is the essential basis of quantum dynamics and dialectics also.

In the evolution of life, of history and of human thought, development, change, or progress makes its appearance by the negation or destruction of what exists. Of necessity, and because of their very nature as the conservative, the resisting, the preserving side of what exists, idealism and the view of *understanding* always sided with the established order of the time, while dialectics represented the revolutionary side, because dialectics denies the stability or the permanence of what exists. This is so because idealism and the view of *understanding* cannot comprehend *change,* except that from an *impulse from without.* For them the world and God who created it (the first cause), aim at *preservation of what exists and at unchanging continuance.* For idealism*, existence* is not real it is only an *appearance,* an *illusion (maya)* and that what is *real* does not exist. The *real* is the ethereal realm, the *universal* of Plato, where there is absolute order, permanence and perfection"

---

5. Heisenberg, W. "Atomic Physics and Causal Law" in *The Physicists Conception of Nature* (1958). Also, la nature dans la physique contemporaine, tr. from German by A.E. Leroy, Éditions Gallimard, (1962)

Hegel (1770-1831 AD) readopted dialectics of Heraclitus as the principal tool of philosophy and brought an all-round development of it in an idealistic form. He claimed that the essence of all previous philosophy is preserved, absorbed and sublated in his own system, because he made explicit what was implicit in them all. An excellent exposition of this theme and that of Hegel's philosophy is given by W.T. Stace[6].

Hegel deduced the laws of dialectics from the history of nature, of society and of thought. Engels summarized these laws as follows [7]:

1. The law of the transformation of quantity to quality and vice versa;
2. The law of the interpenetration of opposites;
3. The law of the negation of the negation;"

Hegel's dialectical method stands in contrast on the one hand to what he called raisonnement of old philosophy and on the other, to the geometrical method of Descartes and Spinoza.

"Raisonnement" is the conventional mode of thought, which begins with some arbitrarily selected facts or reflections such as the *universals* for Plato or the *categories* for Kant and then builds conclusion based on them. No definite or certain conclusion is ever possible from such random and arbitrarily selected assumptions or opinions. Descartes and Spinoza tried to correct these defects of old philosophy by adopting the rigorous methods of geometry. Geometry begins with axioms, which are self-evident and necessary truths and proceed by rigorous deductions to draw only those conclusions, which follow by logical necessity. Thus Descartes started with the axiom *"I am"* and Spinoza started with axioms to develop philosophical theorems, the same way as Euclid did with Geometry. What they in

---

*This ethereal realm of Plato from which this universe arose through a *big bang* (the first impulse or the first cause) is the object of investigation of *official* theoretical science. Our senses cannot perceive this unchanging realm, it can only be comprehended through mathematics and through thought alone.

6. W.T. Stace, "The Philosophy of Hegel", Dover Publications, Inc., (1955).
7. F. Engels, "Dialectics of Nature", International Publishers, N.Y. p 26 (1940).

reality tried to do was to give a more materialistic basis to "raisonnement".

Hegel also wanted to abolish mere opinion and attain certainty by rigorous logical methods, but he rejected the geometrical methods of Descartes and Spinoza: *"That these methods, however indispensable and brilliantly successful in their own province, are unserviceable for philosophical cognition is self-evident. They have presuppositions; their style of cognition is that of understanding, proceeding under the canon of formal identity"[8]*.

By *presupposition* Hegel means the axioms, definitions or any other proposition with which philosophy may begin, including the so called *self-evident truths* of geometry, mathematics and natural science. The sun going around a fixed and flat earth was such a *self-evident truth* for example. By *understanding* he characterizes that stage of the development of the mind at which it views everything as immutable and unchanging and it regards the opposites as mutually exclusive and absolutely cut off from each other. The Aristotelian laws of identity, contradiction and the excluded middle are the canons of its procedure.

Until the advent of quantum dynamics in early 20th century, natural science was mainly guided by the view of *understanding*. Even after the overwhelming triumph of quantum dynamics over classical mechanics, *official* natural science still insists on being guided by the view of *understanding* or causality.

Understanding believes that two opposites, such as *being* and *nothing* absolutely exclude each other. Spinoza (1632 – 1677) for example with his concept of "limit" or boundary regarded the infinite and the finite as mutually exclusive opposites. It was therefore, impossible for him to solve the problem how the *finite* could ever issue out of the *infinite*, how infinite God could have any boundary or contact with finite man which would limit God's infiniteness. Thus ancient philosophy always ended up in dualism. It was thought that *many,* proceed out of the *one, is* the *one.* Yet how can that be, since the *many* and the *one* are opposites. The materialists and the pluralists,

---

8. Quoted in "The Logic of Hegel", tr. William Wallace, Claredon Press, Oxford, §231 (1892)

emphasized *multiplicity* while the idealists and the mystics emphasized *unity* but none of them could find a bridge from one to the other.

Understanding meets every question with an inflexible *either------or*, the electron is either a particle or a wave, a thing either "is" or "is not. It sees things and categories as static, immutable, as unchanging, given at one stroke by a creator once for all. Nature and history in this view has only extension in space, but no change or development in time. If there is any change at all, it is cyclic within a narrow confine and always comes back to the same position like the cycle in the seasons. For *understanding* any deduction of a category from another category is impossible. So it cannot explain motion, change and development. It has to take resort to a first impulse, a first cause not from this world but from without, - from God. *Understanding* has no consistent way to explain the development of the world, nature, history, or human thought, except by isolated and narrow causal relation and by the need of an omnipotent and omniscient creator.

Hegel resolved the problem of old philosophy by his principle of the *unity of the opposites* –the dialectical method: the notion that nothing in this world is by itself alone but contains its Siamese twin - its opposite, together in its element. Hegel found that a thing or a concept contain its own opposite hidden within itself and eventually develops to give rise to a conflict. By rational necessity a thesis gives rise to its opposite – the antithesis and so to a contradiction. But reason cannot rest in what is contradictory, and is forced to resolve this to a synthesis. The synthesis contains within itself both the unity and the opposition of the thesis and the antithesis and posits itself as a new thesis and so on. A genus contain its opposite hidden within itself and this opposite acts as the differentia to convert genus to species. Thus the whole of nature, history and thought develop through this triple movement or triad. The entire series of categories is a compulsory process forced onwards by the compelling necessity of reason. This process can never stop. *Being- nothing- becoming* is the first Hegelian triad.

The three laws of dialectics discovered by Hegel represent a comprehensive and an all-inclusive view of the universe and its development from the subatomic to the cosmic. Everything in this world implicitly contains everything else and hence can be derived from each other without the breach of the *fallacy of illicit process* or the principle: *ex nihilo nihil fit* of formal logic, that forbids the derivation of a conclusion which is not present in the premise or a consequent not contained in the antecedent. The universe in this view is a dynamically interconnected whole, which is *self- determined* and where the *end* is logically and implicitly prior to the *beginning* i.e., the end is the true beginning. All change, motion, development in this view proceeds through *nodal points* or leaps (governed by specific laws) where dialectical opposites either mutually annihilate each other or are sublated (*aufheben*) into a new synthesis and so on (the negation of the negation) and where changes in quantity leads to a qualitative change and vice versa.

As Engels pointed out, with the dialectics of Hegel, philosophy in the conventional sense comes to a close. This is because Hegel comprehended the key to the understanding of all development, change and motion in this world and showed a practical way to follow this motion and development in the realm of nature, history and thought. At the same time he proved (although unconsciously) the futility of searching for eternal and absolute truth, which was the aim of all previous philosophy. If everything in this world is a process in eternal change and not a ready-made or a finished product given once for all, then no final and absolute truth is ever to be found. All knowledge is necessarily limited and conditioned by the circumstances and the time in which it was acquired.

"As soon as we have once realized – and in the long run no one has helped us to realize it more than Hegel himself - that the task of philosophy thus stated means nothing but the task that a single philosopher should accomplish that which can only be accomplished by the entire human race in its progressive development – as soon as we realize that, there is an end of all philosophy in the hitherto accepted sense of the word. One leaves alone absolute truth which is unattainable along this path or by any single individual; instead, one

pursues attainable, relative truths along the path of positive sciences, and the summation of this results by means of dialectical thinking."[9]

Marx and Engels put dialectics on a materialistic foundation instead of the idealistic one, on which Hegel first developed it. The development of natural science, particularly, the three great discoveries – the cell, inter-transformation of the various forms of energy & the theory of evolution and also the development of capitalism provided them the objective basis for the extension of Hegel's idealistic dialectics to dialectical materialism. Marx used dialectical materialism to reveal the secrets of the development of the human society – its history and the development of Capital. Together with Engels, they sketched in broad outline the thread of connection that run through nature, the history of mankind and its thought process, - all as the manifestation of *matter in perpetual and eternal motion.*

Thus the intuitive dialectical conception of nature of the ancient Greek thinkers finds its validation in the dialectical materialism of Marx and Engels, but with much richer contents and at a higher level of knowledge provided by the development of the last two and a half thousand years. This is a living example of the Hegelian concept of the *unity of thinking and being* that the objective dialectical process working in nature finds its reflection in the subjective thinking of man.

Natural science, which is the main lever of all knowledge still works in the *metaphysical* mode of thinking and tumbles into the interconnectedness and the laws of development of nature by way of accident. The following view expressed by Mädler, a prominent astronomer, exemplifies the typical thinking of natural scientists at Engels' time: *"All the arrangements of our solar system, so far as we are capable of comprehending them, aim at preservation of what exists and at unchanging continuance. Just as since the most ancient times no animal and no plant on the earth has become more perfect or in any way different, just as we find in all organisms only stages alongside of one another and not following one another, just as our*

---

[9]. F. Engels, "Ludwig Feuerbach" and the Outcome of Classical German Philosophy", International Publishers, N.Y., p. 15 (1941)

own race has always remained the same in corporeal respects – so even the greatest diversity in the co-existing heavenly bodies does not justify us in assuming that these forms are merely different stages of development; it is rather that everything created is equally perfect in itself." quoted by Engels[10]. This view expressed even after the publication of Darwin's theory of evolution, is typical of a science based on the view of *understanding* or causality and it still serves even if unconsciously, as the main guiding principle of *official* natural science.

Engels rightly castigated the natural scientists of his time: *"The first breach in this petrified outlook on nature was made not by a natural scientist but by a philosopher. In 1755 appeared Kant's "Allgemeine Naturgeschichte und Theorie des Himmels [General Natural History and Theory of the Heavens]. The question of the first impulse was abolished; the earth and the whole solar system appeared as something that had* **come into being** *in the course of time. If the great majority of the natural scientists had had a little less of the repugnance to thinking that Newton expressed in the warning: 'Physics, beware of metaphysics!', they would have been compelled from this single brilliant discovery of Kant's to draw conclusions that would have spared them endless deviations and immeasurable amounts of time and labour wasted in false directions. For, Kant's discovery contained the point of departure for all further progress. If the earth was something that had come into being, then its present geological, geographical, and climatic state, and its plants and animals likewise, must be something that had come into being; it must have had a history not only of co-existence in space but also of succession in time. If at once further investigations had been resolutely pursued in this direction, natural science would now be considerably further advanced than it is. But what good could come of philosophy?"*[11].

---

10. Quoted by F. Engels, "Dialectics of Nature", International Publishers, N.Y, p. 8 (1940), *(Mädler, Popular Astronomy , Berlin, 1861, 5th edition, p. 316,*

11. F. Engels, ibid, p. 8 (1940).

The dialectical perspective of the world is an anathema for modern *official* natural science. Traditionally, natural science was concerned with individual things and processes in isolation; it always insisted on precision and clear-cut distinction between objects, cause and effect etc. It was a basic necessity when natural science was at the stage of sorting out things in nature, analyzing its individual parts, studying individual elements and processes in isolation, detached from the whole vast interconnection as fixed, unchanging objects. As such the approach of natural science (the view of *understanding*) was necessary and justified for that time, because without the precision of thought one gets lost in the hazy world of mysticism; this is what distinguished the materialistic West from the spiritual East. But this way of looking at things is too narrowly focused, which fails to comprehend the larger picture, fails to see the forest because of the trees and sooner or later becomes one-sided and limited in scope.

To view things in the larger perspective, in their vast interconnection, in the actual living dynamics of things in their natural environment, in their *coming into being and passing out of existence* (and not as dead species under microscope) is the task of *reason* or dialectics. The truth of *understanding* is only partial, which only have validity in its application to a particular case within a narrow limit of time and space. The sharp line of demarcation imposed by *understanding* is invalid, when one has to consider the totality of things in their manifold and complex interconnections, where the opposites interpenetrate and inter-covert to each other, and where cause and effect inter-change their positions.

This conflict between the views of *understanding* and *reason* is nowhere more acute than in theoretical natural science and in quantum dynamics, where the laws of causality and determinism of classical mechanics break down. In spite all these limitations, *official* natural science still insists on being guided by causality and determinism.

The same blindfoldedness and confusion reins supreme in the field of cosmology also. This remains so even after the trail-blazing dialectical theory of the "*cosmic evolution*" by Immanuel Kant. The Universe willy-nilly came into existence at one single stroke of a magic wand, through a primordial *Big Bang* and this conforms to theological genesis. The highest, that the view of *understanding* or causality could reach so far is the fundamental, the absolute and the ultimate truth of the theory of General Relativity, according to which, matter and space-time is engaged in an eternal and intimate love embrace (space-time warped around matter). This sterile embrace can only have extension, but no change or development of any kind. If according to the *Big Bang* theory, the universe will either expand forever or shrink back to a singularity, what happens then? Does matter change into space at these two extremes? What a sacrilege! One thing transforming into another! Or if matter is only a condensed form of space, then quantity must be changing into quality and vice versa, what a disgrace!

On a less grandeur scale natural science now – after devious winding and random roaming has come to see this development and interconnectedness in nature from the subatomic to the cosmic as a dialectical process. Galaxies, stars and planets *evolve* in time. Under favourable circumstances, the planets evolve further through geological and climatic changes; more highly specific, severely restricted and extremely rare conditions leads to the evolution of life and finally consciousness. All these happen as the interplay of chance and necessity and as the manifestation of matter in motion. In early twentieth century Einstein extended the link between energy (which was known to manifest in many inter-convertible forms) with matter. In retrospect, this link was obvious enough from dialectical point of view alone. If energy is not something extra-material and comes under the concept of matter, then there must be a unity between these two. But natural scientists hardly think in this term, and when by the way of their research they come up with a profound discovery like the "quantum phenomena" or of chance & necessity in evolution, which does not fall under their pet concept of determinism/cause & effect, they tend to distrust their own findings! In this vastness from the galaxies to man, natural science has seen no sign of the invisible hand of a creator – a prejudice that haunted man and a tradition that blunted his vision. Modern *official* theoretical natural science still keeps on hunting for the creator in a realm of perfect order beyond space-time. It thinks in terms of the dichotomy of the view of "understanding", in absolutely rigid and mutually exclusive antithesis of order or chaos, chance or necessity, finite or infinite, multiplicity or unity etc. Order is divine chaos is evil so, the task of theoretical natural science is to look only for order in nature. At the dawn of the modern age, natural science emancipates itself from the spell of theology and begins with a one sided emphasis on the multiplicity and empiricism of old materialism. It achieved a lot along the way, but now finds itself back in the blind alley of theology and idealism.

But what's of post-Hegelian philosophy? If natural science, in spite of its phenomenal achievements still finds itself begging at the door of theology, it has the satisfaction of seeing philosophy sink lower still. Modern philosophy maintains (as Engels put it) *a pseudo existence in the state appointed academia, where, position-hunting, cobweb-spinning eclectic flea-crackers occupy the chairs of philosophy.* Instead of looking for profound truths in the wide world of nature and human society like their predecessors, these namesakes either work openly as the apologists of monopoly capitalism or look inwards to "self" (existentialism) or to *language* (linguistic philosophy) etc. ad nauseam to hunt for absolute truth.

Stephen Hawking is absolutely right when he says: *"In the eighteenth century, philosophers considered the whole of human knowledge, including science, to be their field and discussed questions such as: Did the universe have a beginning? However, in the nineteenth and twentieth centuries, science became too technical and mathematical for philosophers, or anyone else except a few specialists. Philosophers reduced the scope of their inquiries so much that Wittgenstein, the most famous philosopher of this century, said, 'The sole remaining task for philosophy is the analysis of language.' What a comedown from the great tradition of philosophy from Aristotle to Kant!"* [12].

But it is modern natural science that is hiding its bankruptcy and confusion under the mystery of mathematics and like an ostrich is burying its head in the sand of causality and determinism. The philosophy of Heraclitus, Kant, Hegel and Marx means nothing to it. Modern natural science, has come under total subjugation of monopoly capital, and has dishonoured the great tradition set by

---

12. S Hawking, "A Brief History of Time", Bantam Books, p. 174-175 (1990)

Copernicus, Galileo and Darwin. A natural science, which was once inspired by the revolutionary bourgeoisie and created these giants of science, has now become a lap dog of reactionary monopoly capitalism. Modern natural science wants to bring back the absolutist and obscurantist science of feudalism to serve the interest of moribund monopoly capital. It is churning up a "complete theory" of exquisite mathematical beauty and of absolute validity for all eternity, a theory, which is not empirically verifiable. Like modern official philosophy, present day natural science has reduced its scope to mere application of the absolute truth it has attained in the realm of nature. Only those facts that conform to this truth are of interest to science, those that do not, remains in the realms of the Creator or at best are Kantian "thing in itself". Thus we have not only a "comedown from the great tradition of philosophy" but a comedown from the great tradition of natural science too.

THE MAGIC OF MATHEMATICS

Idealization of Mathematics is attributed to Pythagoras. For him *"number is the essence of all things, and the organization of the universe as a whole in its determination is a harmonious system of numbers and their relations"* (Aristotle, *Metaphysics*, I, 5 passim) [1].

Plato formalized this principle of Pythagoras in his philosophy, where mathematics along with the universals was placed in a world beyond space and time and in a realm higher than this world, a realm that our senses cannot perceive. The higher realm, which is presented to thought alone; is the unchanging reality, where there is perfection, permanence and absolute order. Plato's ideas were later incorporated in Christian theology. The ethereal ideals of Plato, which became the dominant notions of mathematics also, continue to be the quasi-official philosophy of modern science. Implicit in this notion is the belief that the universe was created according to a mathematical scheme by some supernatural being or God.

After the idealization and thereby the alienation of mathematics by the Greeks, its development in Europe, particularly, during the medieval fundamentalist Christian period came to a virtual standstill. Meanwhile, the Muslim Arabs continued the traditions of Egyptian, Sumerian, Mesopotamian and Indian civilizations in developing mathematical methods as a tool in their studies of astronomy, architecture, mechanics, etc. leading to the development of the decimal notation, modern Indo-Arabic numeral system and algebra.
The bourgeois democratic revolution in Europe ushered in by the *burgers* and the *journey men* in the later half of fifteenth century, of necessity, gave rise to an unprecedented impetus to the development of natural science, particularly the mechanics of the heavenly and terrestrial bodies and along with it mathematics (its most fundamental elements), culminating in the development of calculus by Leibniz and Newton. From the very start, this revolution was seeded with the materialism, and with the wealth of the mathematical systems developed by the Arabs. This revolution was directed not only against

---

1. Quoted by F. Engels in "Dialectics of Nature", Translated by Clemans Dutt, International Publishers, p. 246 (1940).

the feudal nobility and the church, but also against all idealism and the ethereal notions of reality & mathematics of Plato. Further developments in fluid & wave mechanics, thermo & electro dynamics, geometry, group & set theories etc. and finally the theories of relativity at the beginning of twentieth century brought the so-called classical mechanics to a close. The conclusion of this period also coincides with the winding down of the bourgeois democratic revolution in Europe and the rise of parasitic monopoly finance capitalism.

The development of quantum dynamics in early twentieth century with its notion of uncertainty, unity of the opposites, lack of determinism etc in direct contradiction of classical mechanics, revolutionized natural science and technology. Even after about a century of breadth taking development of quantum dynamics, the old mechanics with its mathematics and laws of determinism, continuity, causality etc. personalized by Newton and Einstein still rule natural science. Quantum dynamics is considered as an aberration, as weird, "spooky" and as a fringe phenomenon.

The stunning success of the theories of relativity in early 20th century, led Einstein to revive Pythagoras's notion of mathematics. *"How can it be"* he wondered, *"that mathematics being a product of human thought which is independent of experience, is so admirably appropriate to the objects of reality?"*[2].

The general theory of relativity is a classic example where the power of mathematics, pure thought and aesthetics devoid of any empirical content is purported to have conceived the ultimate reality of the universe. *"Our experience hitherto justifies us in believing that nature is the realization of the simplest conceivable mathematical ideas. I am convinced that we can discover by means of purely mathematical constructions the concepts and the laws connecting them with each other, which furnish the key to the understanding of natural phenomena. ... In a certain sense, therefore, I hold it true that pure*

---

2. A. Einstein, "Sidelights on Relativity", Dover, N.Y., p. 28 (1983).

thought can grasp reality, as the ancients dreamed", declares Albert Einstein [3]

Einstein with the active support from Arthur Eddington, set the idealist tone of *"official"* theoretical science that was to follow the theory of general relativity. Eddington like his compatriot Isaac Newton was adept at manipulative skills and was the darling of the British imperial establishment of his time, while on the contrary other scientists like Charles Darwin or J.B.S. Haldane for example, whose theories were at odds with the established order were always persecuted by the state. Einstein actively pursued and promoted the mystical notion of mathematics, violently rejecting quantum dynamics - a branch of physics, which he helped to create. This great mind of the twentieth century virtually insulated himself against the later developments in physics, particularly quantum dynamics and spent the last thirty years of his later life in a jungle of mathematical constructions in a vain search of a unified theory of gravity and electromagnetism and in attempts to undermine the quantum theory. He insisted on the rationalist notions of certainty, determinism, symmetry, continuity etc., based on a "continuous field" concept of the objective reality, which were later incorporated in quantum dynamics to make it free of its "spookiness".

For his frenzied followers in theoretical physics, mathematics is not any more a mere tool of scientific enquiry, but rather it is an *"a priori"* determinant of the universe. Theoretical Physics, particularly modern cosmology has become a field of dazzling fireworks of mathematics. It no longer feels constrained by experimentation and/or the vagaries of empirical facts. A sense of beauty, symmetry and the *"free creation of the mind"* are all that is needed to find the ultimate truth of this world and a *Theory of Everything*. *"Beauty before truth"*[4] is its slogan. The general theory of relativity and the *"Big Bang"*

---

3. A. Einstein, "Essays in Science", Translated by Alan Harris from "Mein Weltbild, Quedro Verlag, Amsterdam, (1933), The Wisdom Library, N.Y., p. 16 – 17 (1934).

4. A. Zee, "Fearful Symmetry, The Search for Beauty in Modern Physics", MacMillan Pub. Company, N.Y., p. 3 (1986).

creation of the universe that follow from this theory is the final and ultimate truth and all reality has to conform to this truth.

Modern cosmology has finally been able to glimpse the ultimate reality - it is there! Like the huge pile of a scrambled jigsaw puzzle; the inherent perfection, the beauty of the *absolute reality* are hidden in the heap of broken and scrambled -symmetries that is our present world. If we can fit all the pieces in the right places again we will be able to reconstruct the face of God and of the original *absolute reality* and in the process we will discover *the theory of everything.* "The task of physics" declares Steven Weinberg a prominent physicist, *"is to see through the appearances down to the underlying, very simple, symmetric reality"* [5]. But how do we proceed in the absence of solid empirical facts, some of which are impossible to obtain and will forever remain impossible for us? As Stephen Hawking[6] assures us: *"... the requirements of mathematical consistency will lead us to a complete unified theory within the lifetime of some of us who are around today..."* Such is the certainty with which modern physicists talk of reality – a realm that we can reach through mathematics and by thought alone.

According to idealist Hegel, nature is the alienation, a miserable copy; the *otherness* of the *Absolute Idea.* This *Absolute Idea* comes to self-realization and to itself again through the philosophy of Hegel. Exactly the same way for our physicists, this world is the vulgarization, the broken heap of the *Absolute Beauty* and eternal reality, which can be comprehended and brought back to itself again through thought, by following the *requirements of mathematical consistency.*

Thus mathematics tells us that this universe emerged from a state of perfect symmetry (perhaps of Platonic realm) into this rubble-dirt of broken symmetries. Everything in this universe, bosons, fermions etc. including us are shards of a ten or a twenty-six dimensional *space* of perfect symmetry broken to this heap of rubbish, by *Higgs fields.*

---

5. Quoted by Timothy Ferris in "The Whole Shebang", Simon & Shuster, p. 215 (1997).
6. S. Hawking, "A Brief History of Time", Bantam Books, p. 167 (1990)

Based on mathematics alone the physicists can confirm this truth and can give an *eyewitness* account of the events that followed the primordial explosion back up to the one millionth of a trillionth of a trillionth of a trillionth of a second (Planck time).

Like the Genesis, this world including us, and all that *exist* therefore owe their existence to an *original sin - the negation of perfection*. Modern theoretical science therefore, provides a mathematical verification of the Genesis. Theology thus finds itself vindicated after all these years of abuse in the hands of Copernican, Galilean and Darwinian science, the truth have finally prevailed! By the way, this whole exercises of theoretical natural science unfortunately, inadvertently though, brings out an ugly truth of Hegelian dialectics also: *the portentous power of the negative*. We poor mortals after all owe our existence in the negation of perfection – due to broken symmetries. In a *perfectly symmetrical reality nothing can exist!* Since according to the Eleatics, *existence is not real and that what is real does not exist.*

But why all these hymns and songs about perfect symmetry, beauty and *a priority* of mathematics? Starting from Immanuel Kant we now know that the galaxies, stars etc. *evolved* from swirling mass of gas and matter particles clumping together by chance encounter and by the force of gravity. These random and chaotic collisions are anything but beautiful and so is the case with the brutal world of geology, biology and society. At some fundamental level nature is only approximately symmetrical (isospin), and in some basic processes like β-particle decay, symmetry is not preserved at all. Asymmetry and the unity of the opposites are supposed to prevail in the most fundamental units of matter such as protons and mesons. The holy grail of modern cosmology – the *big bang* (if true) violated symmetry, since only matter and no antimatter, was produced as a result. The holiest of the holy namely light (photons) is a composite unity of the opposites of matter and antimatter and at certain energy equivalent to the total mass can be resolved in to a particle and an antiparticle like the electron/positron pair at ~ 1.02 MeV of the photon energy.

Modern theoretical physics only want to see the static beauty and perfect-ness in nature and not the ugliness of random, chaotic processes; precisely because that is what mathematics demands and can deal with! When faced with the fact that *parity* is violated in every single process involving weak interaction, the boisterous worshipers of perfect symmetry just mumble. The self-proclaimed disciple of Einstein, Anthony Zee [7] has the audacity to proclaim: *"The reader probably wants to ask why nature violates parity, well, who knows? Nature, like the gorilla in the classic joke does what She pleases. I am among a group of physicists who still feel that nature **should** respect parity"*. This is at best a poor consolation for bad science.

Long before Herr Einstein and company, one Herr Eugen Dühring was making exactly similar claims about the *a priori* validity of pure mathematics. Engels, in his Anti-Dühring thoroughly refuted these absurd claims about mathematics and put forward the dialectical materialistic view:

"But it is not at all true that in pure mathematics the mind deals only with its own creations and imaginations. The concepts of number and form have not been derived from any source other than the world of reality. The ten fingers on which men learnt to count, that is, carry out the first arithmetical operation, may be anything else, but they are certainly not a free creation of the mind. Counting requires not only objects that can be counted, but also the ability to exclude all properties of the objects considered other than their number – and this ability is the product of a long historical evolution based on experience. Like the idea of number, so the idea of form is derived exclusively from the external world, and does not arise in the mind as a product of pure thought. ... But in order to make it possible to investigate these forms and relations in their pure state, it is necessary to abstract them entirely from their content, to put the content aside as irrelevant; hence we get the point without dimensions, lines without breadth, and thickness, a and b and x and y, constants and variables;

---

7. A. Zee, "Fearful Symmetry, The Search for Beauty in Modern Physics", MacMillan Pub. Company, N.Y., p. 45 (1986).

and only at the very end of all these do we reach for the first time the free creations and imaginations of the mind, that is to say imaginary magnitudes. Even the apparent derivation of mathematical magnitudes from each other does not prove their a priori origin, but only their rational interconnection. ... Like all other sciences, mathematics arose out of the need of man; from measurement of land and of the content of vessels, from computation of time & mechanics. But, as in every department of thought, at a certain stage of development the laws abstracted from the real world become divorced from the real world and are set over against it as something independent, as laws coming from outside to which the world has to conform. This took place in society and in the state, and in this way, and not otherwise, pure mathematics is subsequently applied to the world, although it is borrowed from this same world and only represents one section of its forms of interconnection – and it is only just precisely because of this that it can be applied at all" [8].

After loudly beating the drums of *pure thought*, and *a priory* validity of mathematics Einstein says exactly the opposite as if in a whisper or as a footnote, in reference to Galileo: *"Pure logical thinking cannot yield us any knowledge of the empirical world, all knowledge of reality starts from experience and ends in it. Propositions arrived at by purely logical means are completely empty as regards reality. Because Galileo saw this, and particularly because he drummed it into the scientific world, he is the father of modern physics – indeed of modern science altogether"*[9]. And on his own theory of relativity: *"I consider it quite possible that physics cannot be based on the field concept, i.e., continuous structure. In that case, nothing remains of my entire castle in the air, gravitation theory included, (and of) the rest of modern physics "*[10]. So, which Einstein are we to believe?

---

8. F. Engels, "Herr Eugen Dühring's Revolution in Science (Anti Dühring), International Publishers N.Y., p. 45-46 (1939).

9. A. Einstein, "Essays in Science", ", Translated by Alan Harris from "Mein Weltbild, Quedro Verlag, Amsterdam, (1933), The Wisdom Library, N.Y., p.14 (1934).

10. A. Pais, Subtle is the Lord ... " *The Science and the Life of Albert Einstein"*, Oxford University Press, (1982) 465..

There is no a-priority in the mathematical formulation of theories of natural science! The forms of the mathematical relations and their parameters do not automatically follow from some *first principles* but are arbitrarily put there to conform to empirical facts. Einstein must have considered innumerable geometrical forms and relations before finding that Riemannian geometry of curbed space and the concept of warped space-time suits his purpose of explaining the equivalence of gravitational and kinetic mass. There may yet be other mathematical relations that can explain this equivalence equally well.

Mathematics like all other branches of theoretical knowledge has its own rule and internal relation once it is *abstracted* from empirical experience and becomes *"independent"* of it. Ever newer internal relations can be deduced out of the old ones and so on, conditioned by the epoch, the mental set-up and the power of intuition of individual mathematicians.

Just as in language, arts and music, with some simple elements & forms an infinite variations can be made and with a small collection of such elements and forms an infinite range of literature, arts and music can be composed, so in mathematics an infinite *free creations of the mind* can be accomplished. But that does not necessarily mean that these simple elements and forms do not have empirical origin! Of the infinite range of mathematical *creations*, natural scientists *use* only those that help them to systematize facts and empirical experience. Thus, group & set theories, Riemannian geometry to name a few were the *free creations* of mathematicians before natural science found use for them. Traditionally, natural science always deals with approximate data, and *use* mathematical functions to depict and systematize reality and empirical experience. It continually fine-tunes the mathematical forms and relations to accommodate ever newer and more refined observations

The present *official* theoretical physicists churn out mathematical relations with rampant abandon and try to impose these on nature. In their *free creation of the mind* and with their *logical consistency of mathematics* of classical mechanics they set no limit to the flight of their imagination. They forget the fact that there is a gulf of difference between the *pure* mathematics, whose program is the *exact* deduction of consequences from logically independent postulates, and the *applied* mathematics of *approximation* needed for science. Natural science uses approximate empirical data, which can be fitted on in various ways to *analytic functions* of *pure* mathematics, but the results are only valid in a narrow range of the data values for the argument. The *analytic functions*, i.e., those whose Taylor's series converge in the neighbourhood of a given point have *precise* mathematical properties and *smoothness*. It is very easy for an idealist with *aesthetic* sense to assume that in nature only *analytic functions* present themselves. Just as Georg Cantor in his attempts to prove his continuum hypothesis had to make a distinction between *consistent* and *inconsistent* collections; according to him only the former were *sets*, the latter (such as the collection of all the sets or of all the ordinals) were not. Cantor called the *inconsistent* collections the *absolute infinite* that God alone could know.

Another property of the analytic functions, which impresses the worshipers of beauty and *aesthetic* is that, such functions are known for all values of their argument when their values in any small range of the argument values are known. Thus, the proposition that the laws of nature involve *analytic functions* leads to a complete mechanistic determination of the world based on their experimentally determined value in a narrow range only. But the validity of such a procedure to use mathematics in the realm of macrocosm and microcosm was questioned both by philosophers such as Bridgman [11] and scientists like Klein [12] at the advent of quantum mechanics. The Quantum Uncertainty Principle shows the folly of such an enterprise because a great many of the difficulties in applying classical mechanics to quantum phenomena lies in this kind of naïve and over-simplified application of idealized mathematics to the real world. Classical mechanics demands continuity, determinism, sharpness, predictability, precision, smoothness, causality, certainty, etc., in other words *self-evident truths* and "good old common sense" experienced in everyday life in the finite world. But as quantum dynamics and dialectics amply

---

11. P.W. Bridgman, "The logic of Modern Physics" The Macmillan Co., (1927).
12. F. Klein, "Elementarmathematik vom Höheren Standpunkt aus", Vol. 3, Berlin, (1924)

demonstrate such a view of objective reality is untenable even in the finite scale.

The same situation applies to the extension of the *concepts* and *measurements* to macrocosm and microcosm that modern physics uses based on the experience in the finite scale. What level of confidence can we have when a physicist uses the concept of *mass* or *dimension* of a quark for example or when a cosmologist describes the primordial atom before the *big bang* and its immediate aftermath, the mind boggling *inflation* etc, based on the extension of mathematical relations obtained through experiments in the laboratory and in an Euclidian space? Experimental evidence accumulated so far already questions the validity of such a procedure. The formal mass-energy concept break down in the case of recently discovered *"mystery meson"* (X3872). In the case of *pi-meson* or *pion*, an *up* and *antidown* quark combination has a mass-energy of only 140 MeV (million electron volt), yet the same quark combination (but only with different spin) in a *rho-meson* has a mass-energy of 770 MeV!

The experience of natural science in astrophysics, all terrestrial sciences and now in the quantum world shows that the objective reality is exactly opposite to what was conceived by our old, prejudiced and historically conformed "common sense" of causality; but instead, are governed by dialectical laws of development. That blind and arbitrary randomness, accidents, chances, chaos etc. rule the world, but while on the surface arbitrariness hold sway, there are zones of regularity, order, necessity etc. that assert themselves and are always governed by inner, hidden laws. The task of science is to *discover* these laws and not to *impose* laws on nature manufactured by the *"free creation"* of the mind. The world-views of classical mechanics and quantum dynamics are therefore incompatible and are mutually exclusive in the sense of classical mechanics. Any attempts to bridge the gap between the two, such as quantum gravity, hidden variable etc. theories are bound to fail. One can therefore, appreciate the outrage of an idealist scientist like Albert Einstein towards quantum dynamics and the inability of modern theoretical physics to reconcile it with classical mechanics. What classical mechanics is to old materialism so is quantum mechanics to dialectical materialism.

Based on the *free creation of the mind & mathematical consistency*; *official* cosmologists bring out science fiction dressed in mathematics in an attempt to establish the *absolute truth* of the theory of general relativity and the *big bang* theory. Like spiritual Gurus and priests they play with words, speak a volume (with mathematics), but which in reality means absolutely nothing. We are just as wise with it as without it. Thus we have theories of inflation, super gravity, super strings, 26 dimensional reality, infinite number of universes etc. etc., garbed in dizzying mathematics, but which for ever will remain beyond human experience. Kant's category of the *thing in itself* sounds like a child's play compared to this! A *theory of everything* that can be invoked any time, any place and in any situation is totally useless for any practical purpose. If such a theory is needed, theology already provided us one of the purest kinds: *everything in this universe happens due to the will of God*. This works without fail! Why spend time, energy and most of all resources of society to create yet another one?

Modern theoretical physics and cosmology are turned into absurd myth making machines, fueled by idealized mathematics to replace moribund theology. This sorry state of affairs for natural science is due to its reactionary retreat led by Albert Einstein to the mathematical idealism of the early Greeks; in the face of the development of revolutionary quantum dynamics. Its chief defect is the adoption of the Greek idealist notion that space and time has tangible ontological reality. Materialist and dialectical philosophers starting from Democritus denied the ontological validity of space and time and considered these as abstracted entities arising from commonsense life experience. Einstein, erroneously ascribed quality, quantity, measure etc. empirical categories to things that have no real existence! As a result theoretical physics and cosmology are now harvesting all these fantastic and absurd notions of the cosmos and the paradoxes that the early Greeks, particularly Zeno faced.

The only way natural science can rid itself of the myths and fantasies created by Einsteinian cosmology, is by adopting the criteria of knowledge set by Karl Marx: "*The question whether objective truth can be attributed to human thinking is not a question of theory but a practical question. In practice man must prove the truth, i.e., the reality and power, the "this-sidedness" of his thinking. The dispute over the reality or non-reality of thinking which is isolated from practice is a purely scholastic question."* Theses on Feuerbach.

EPILOGUE:

Albert Einstein died in 1955, but his theories of relativity remain promoted to the status of invariable truth of the world by monopoly capitalism. Like theology these theories are used as a rational/moral justification for its rule and to explain the details of all known natural phenomena and any newly discovered ones. Einstein's failed efforts to build a "unified theory" of all the forces of nature (gravitational, electromagnetic and nuclear) in one grand theory have become the primary preoccupation of modern official physics. The "spooky" quantum dynamics so much reviled by Einstein; but which became overwhelmingly successful, is now tamed within the concept of his "continuous field" by his successors; who continue to pursue with much vigor his dream of a "theory of everything" that would bring all the laws of nature under one framework, revealing the "mind of God".

High value research projects funded by monopoly capitalism are subjectively directed to "prove" the esoteric theories of Einstein with increasingly tenuous experiments. The British scientist Arthur Eddington's contested "proof" of the theory of general relativity (GR) set the trend in modern physics. This theory driven enquiry of Nature based on idealized mathematics set modern physics away from materialism, which once was its great merit. This represents a great blow to the revolutionary natural science, which steered humanity through various class and ideological hurdles only to be now co-opted by regressive monopoly capitalism.

But things have started to change. The fundamental weakness of the mathematical idealism and the theories of relativity upon which the virtual edifice of so called "New physics" of Einstein was based is now coming back to haunt it; as physicists now face insurmountable experimental problems in completing the summit of their edifice. The nakedness of the Emperor is now getting exposed in spite of the frenetic efforts by official scientists to dress him up with more and more exotic "dark and black" garments.

The Nobel laureate Steven Weinberg is one of the most prominent representatives of modern official physics and one of the most aggressive advocates of the "Theory of Everything (TOE). The following comment by this author was posted in the Guardian in a review article of Weinberg's book "Dreams of a Final Theory" by Tim Radford. This booklet like the comment below constitutes a rebuttal and a negation of the priests of modern official physics like Weinberg.

"Dream of a Final Theory will always remain a dream and will end as an official scientific enterprise either with the collapse of monopoly capitalism, or a final fiasco in the hunt for the God particle (a theory of everything); whichever comes first.

There is no final truth or final theory to be reached! No "mind of God" to be known! Dialectics in the person of Heraclitus (and in direct contradiction to Greek idealism, causality and "good old common sense") came to this conclusion centuries ago. According to dialectics everything is in constant change, as a result of inner strife, is in an unending process of *"coming into being and passing out of existence"*; in other words *"**change**"* is the only category that is permanent and absolute. The development of natural science throughout history is a vindication of this fact.

Just as Nature or the universe (ontologically) is incapable of reaching a final, ever lasting, unchanging or an ideal state, so is thought (which is only a reflection of Nature in the mind of man) epistemologically is incapable of comprehending a completed, exhaustive or immutable knowledge - the so-called final truth of the world. Dialectics only allows iterative, ever-better relative truths in an infinite progression, without ever coming to a termination or reaching an absolute or final truth.

This priestly practice of searching for the final theory by Prof. Weinberg et al., in particle physics and in cosmology and the related reductionism in biological (the selfish genes) and social sciences (positivism) is a legacy of what Hegel called the "view of understanding" and causality of ancient Greek idealism, theology, rationalism and classical materialism. These were all based on the ideology of various dominant social classes that cherished an elusive permanent existence.

This reactionary idealist tendency was incorporated in (other wise revolutionary) natural science, through the mathematical idealism of Albert Einstein at the turn of the 20th century; after the collapse of Newtonian mechanics and classical materialism. It was a reaction to the revolutionary developments in natural and social sciences i.e., the theory of evolution, quantum mechanics and Marxism, all of which have their basis in dialectics.

With the decline of theology in the Western World, monopoly capitalism has adopted Einsteinian mathematical idealism and is promoting it, primarily as a prop to its rule. Monopoly capitalism has totally expropriated natural science. Idealist theories now exclusively guide the search for knowledge. The role of natural science now like that of theology is to interpret and to reveal the truth of its theories in the details of Nature. Physics is reduced to preaching theology!! It is indeed the "End of Physics".

APPENDIX 1

A SELECTED LIST OF PHILOSOPHERS & THINKERS

Thale	(~580 B.C.)
Pythagorous of Samoa	(580 (?) – 520 B.C.)
Heraclitus	(544 – 483 B.C.)
Permenides	(515 – 450 B.C.)
Leucippus of Meletas	(~440 B.C.)
Democritus of Addera	(~420 B.C.)
Socrates	(470 – 399 B.C.)
Plato	(429 – 347 B.C.)
Aristotle	(384 – 322 B.C.)
Epicurus	(341 – 270 B.C.)
Lucretius	(~100 - ~55 B.C.)
Copernicus, Nicolas	(1473 – 1543 A.D.
Luther, Martin	(1483 – 1546 A.D.)
Bruno, Giordano	(1548 – 1600 A.D.)
Bacon, Francis	(1561 – 1626 A.D.)
Galileo, Galilei	(1564 – 1642 A.D.)
Calvin, John	(1509 – 1604 A.D)
Servetus, Michael	(1511 – 1553 A.D.)
Kepler, Johannes	(1571 – 1630 A.D.)
Gassendi, Pierre	(1592 – 1655 A.D.)
Decartes, Rene	(1596 – 1650 A.D.)
Spinoza, Benedict	(1632 – 1677 A.D.)
Locke, John	(1632 – 1704 A.D.)
Malebranche, Nicolas	(1638 – 1715 A.D.)
Newton, Isaac	(1642 – 1727 A.D.)
Leibniz, G.W.	(1646 – 1716 A.D.)
Bayle, Pierre	(1647 – 1706 A.D.)
Berkeley, George	(1685 – 1753 A.D.)
Voltaire, J.F.	(1694 – 1774 A.D.)
Hume, DavId	(1711 – 1776 A.D.)
Rousseau, J.J.	(1711 – 1775 A.D.)
Diderot, Denis	(1713 – 1784 A.D.)
Helvetius	(!715 – 1771 A.D.)
Kant, Immanuel	(1724 – 1804 A.D.)
Lamarck, J.B.	(1744 – 1829 A.D.)
Hegel, G.W.F	(1770 – 1831 A.D.)

Comte, Auguste	(1798 – 1857 A.D.)
Oken, Lorenz	(1779 – 1851 A.D.)
Schelling, Fieddrich	(1775 – 1854 A.D.)
Darwin, Charles	1809 – 1882 A.D.)
Ludwig Feuerbach	(1804 – 1872 A.D.)
Marx, Karl	(1818 – 1883 A.D.)
Engels, Frederick	(1820 – 1895 A.D.)
Lenin, V.I.	(1870 – 1924 A.D.)
Mach, Ernst	(1838 – 1916 A.D.)
Planck, Max	(1858 – 1947 A.D.)
Eddington, Aurther	(1882 – 1944 A.D.)
Einstein, Albert	(1879 – 1955) A.D.)
Bohr, Niels	(1885 – 1962 A.D.)
Heisenberg, Werner	(1901 – 1976 A.D.)

The chief philosophical and scientific defect of so-called "New Physics" and cosmology– associated with Albert Einstein; lies in its regress to the naive and the commonsense conception of space, time, and the infinite of classical Greek mathematical idealism. Materialist philosophers since Democritus, dialectical philosophers since Epicurus and the rationalist philosophers like Leibniz, Kant and Hegel, all contended that space and time are abstractions and epistemological thought/mathematical objects that have no ontological (physical) existence; so one cannot relate quantity, quality, measure etc., - in one word empirical concepts with such abstract entities. For them space and time has circumlocutory meaning only in the context matter in uninterrupted motion.

The old (Newtonian) physics mainly dealt with material things and their motion, change evolution etc. and considered space and time as the background or the stage in which matter plays out its role. "New Physics" and cosmology on the contrary, assigns an ontological reality to space and time (a four-dimensional "spacetime" virtual structure), which presupposes a beginning of the universe, which is limited both in spatial and temporal extension. The theory of General Relativity (GR) of Albert Einstein is therefore a multidimensional modified Riemannian geometrical construct rather than a theory of physics. This necessarily has led to many paradoxes and fantastic speculations for "New Physics" as was the case with Zeno. As a result modern theoretical physics and cosmology has become fields of futile exercise in the abstraction of the abstraction based only on the "consistency" of mathematics without any relevance to reality.

GR have already been "proved" for the nth times with ever-precise and tenuous experiments and observations. More are underway or planned as the scientific communities around the world celebrate its 100th anniversary. Based on causality and its own adjustable parameters like those of the Ptolemaic epicycles and the theological God, GR has become an absolute truth that can no longer be refuted as long as the "power that be" retains its political and moral authority.

The curious phenomena of hitherto all class society - that of modern monopoly capitalism included - is that the more obscure a ruling "truth", the greater are the efforts made to establish that "truth". Unsurprisingly that "truth" always has its source at the far and the unknown reaches of the cosmos. Real and virtual Temples and Edifices are constructed as the grand monuments of "truth" – Albert Einstein's theory of General Relativity (GR) is no exception. GR specifically is a direct reaction against the revolutionary quantum phenomena in physics and more generally against the revolutionary developments in biology and society towards the end of 19th and early 20th century. But enigmatically, after decades-long attempts by himself and others to unify his theory of gravity with Maxwell's electromagnetism; Einstein (in a letter to his friend Besso) made the last prediction of his life: *"I consider it quite possible that physics cannot be based on the field concept, i.e., continuous structure. In that case nothing remains of nothing remains of my entire castle in the air, gravitation theory included (and of) the rest of modern physics"* A. Pais, Subtle is the Lord ... " *The Science and the Life of Albert Einstein"*, Oxford University Press, (1982) 467,

This booklet and other works by Dr. Malek is a daring and a highly controversial attempt to counter the idealist worldview of modern official physics and cosmology; by positing a materialist dialectical perspective that might ironically vindicate the last prediction/prophesy of Albert Einstein!

Dr. Abdul Malek is a retired Canadian scientist, a non-affiliated thinker and a writer, who advocates the use of materialist dialectics as a tool of enquiry in the realm of cosmology, physical and biological sciences. He follows the pioneering lead of Frederick Engels in his scientific works. Dr. Malek also greatly values the personal inspiration of (Late) Prof. Halton (Chip) Arp and his radical views and revolutionary discoveries in the realm of astronomy, astrophysics and cosmology. Dr. Malek is the author of numerous journal articles and books on a dialectical approach to quantum dynamics and cosmology, including "The Dialectical Universe". He lives in Montreal.

www.ingramcontent.com/pod-product-compliance
Lightning Source LLC
Chambersburg PA
CBHW071414040426
42444CB00009B/2246